Cantos for the Crestfallen

In my idiotic heart, idiocy is singing its head off. I HAVE PREVAILED!

— G. Bataille

CANTOS FOR THE CRESTFALLEN

Pseudo-Leopardi

Translated by

A. Necrezută, F. Pilastru
& I. Imaculată

gnOme

CANTOS FOR THE CRESTFALLEN
© the authors and gnOme books

gnOme books
gnomebooks.wordpress.com

Please address inquiries to:
gnomebooks@gmail.com

Cover: Geertgen tot Sint Jans, "John the Baptist in the Wilderness." Public domain image. Source: http://commons.wikimedia.org/wiki/File:Geertgen_tot_Sint_Jans_004.jpg

ISBN-13: 978-0692218853
ISBN-10: 0692218858

A NOTE ON THE TEXT: The present translation is based on the Romanian manuscript of the *Canti per gli abbattuti*, recently discovered in Brasov. In light of the principle of *lectio difficilior potior*, it is apparent that this manuscript is the source of the 31 poems in the 'Bologna Notebooks' attributed to one Pseudo-Leopardi. This determination lends credence to the theory, espoused by Prof. Enzo Tessaro, that the Bologna Notebooks are the work of a Romanian student attending university in Italy. Because the original manuscript, now housed in the archives of Biroul de Filosofie Muzicală (BFM) in Bucharest, is lacking both title and attribution, these have been retained from the Italian version in order to prevent further editorial confusion. Unlike the Italian version, which is signed "Ps-Leopardi," the Romanian text concludes with the following colophon:

AMOR, mai mult român decât ROMA, me fecit. Fecemi la divina podestate, La somma sapïenza e 'l primo amore . . . Lasciate ogni speranza, voi ch'entrate. Fericirea noastră, a modernilor, este că ne-am descoperit infernal în suflet. A FI (esse) + Tau (tristitia) = FIAT.

III + I

After this, on the final page, is a drawing, possibly in another hand, of a goat atop a spiral column (reproduced on the following page).

The translators would like to thank the BFM for its generous support of their work. "For blessed is not he who begins a thing and does not finish it, but blessed is he who says and does and accomplishes good . . . Here is the tomb in which I lie; take me then, and depart" (Anonymous).

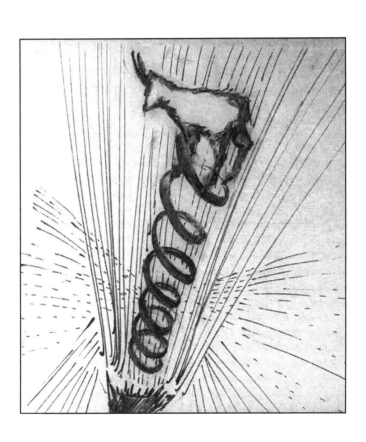

I

Unable to swim the ocean of each other's eyes
We must sit side by side, gazing at a blind world
Whose dumb mouth has lost all taste for silence.

Heads dizzy as ours naturally lean together,
Kept from falling off only by the golden sighs
Suspending these bodies like puppet strings.

The soft tautness of the secret lines is thinning us,
Sweetly drawing all life-feeling inward and up
Into something pulling strongly from far above.

There is no doubt that the sigh-threads will one day
Draw our hearts right through the tops of our heads,
Eventually turning everything totally inside out.

Already my body is something much less my own,
As if the thought of your form is my new skeleton
And your memory of my flesh your new strength.

If I embrace you my own power would crush me
And if you cling to me I would surely evaporate.
Dying lovers do not touch without touching suicide.

Side by side we float and stand. It is our way of lying
Bound together across space on this lost world
Whose eyes will not survive seeing us face to face.

II

The sun that warms this rotting, blooming earth
Knows nothing of the blazing death which scorches
The summit of things where I first wept for you.

Yet still I call it sun, name brightness what I cannot
Look upon without dying, call annihilation what
I cannot not expire from by weeping and sighing for.

What made me both think of bottling those drops
And never really consider doing so? Who made me
Know the melodrama even more true at its falsest?

Later that day none of us needed relics to weep over,
When our silly bodies were a secret golden ossuary,
And witty laughter the worst sorrow we could stomach.

A sweetest meal of sighs we made. Now the asymptotic
Leftovers infinitely remain around the earth like seeds
Of a new life that lives everywhere except this world.

A life not living, more a truly breathless realm beyond
Beyond, an *al di là* far cooler than any philosopher's,
A place composing each here into the mark of its there.

Yes, it was a sun or special kind of luminous void
That my tears veiled, that I-we walked away toward,
A gold that also the blind must shield their eyes from.

III

As if there is any time left to fret or scream over this
Sad world which knows nothing of the paradise it is,
This life not for a second real enough even to deny.

As if my worn out heart has not already despaired
Again for the last time and let the worst do its worst,
Watching corpses bury corpses just for the fun of it.

As if the sigh you thought you lost did not return
Before the next from the widest sphere and joining it
Infinitely accelerate the shrinking of the very cosmos.

As if these and all other things were not already true,
Forever abandoned in the victory no one can win—
Abyss where falling is a blow from which none recover.

So let us listen rather to what neither has nor will occur,
To what never entered the world and solely by not
Entering made a strange appearance around us.

So let us point to the haloes over each other's heads
Precisely where their brilliance is no different from
The supreme impossibility of that silent pointing.

So let us do everything at once while there is still time.
Otherwise I see no reason for keeping up appearances,
For bothering to be, for taking even my last breath.

IV

At night I know you are with me because my spirit
Is shallow in a deeper way, like an infant's breath
Hovering through little holes at the edge of worlds.

Sometimes words speak in my head, verbs not my own
Which say nothing other than their sheer speaking—
Perfect invitations providing no conceivable address.

Even if I delude myself these silent voices are still
The real shadows of your thoughts, of whatever is
Now passing through your mind while I fall asleep.

For I have sewn you into myself with the strong thread
Of your sighs, sealed my eyes to yours with unwept tears,
And let my blood melt with the heat of your heart's light.

It is not your fault that nothing will again make sense.
But you are to blame that it will now forever appear
To be your fault. Forgiveness lies in my lack of thanks.

You are that whereby nothing ever coincides with itself.
You are that whereby blackness sees more than light.
You are that whereby sorrow is the immeasurable joy.

As our bodies will never discover a replacement for air,
Likewise this much is known to me, that you are with me
In the dark, truly here in the blind non-truth of night.

V

Not among they who drink from fear of intoxication
Are found these friends, my lost best lovers of the worst.
Their wine is inexistent, classed among the impossibles.

Happy there is nothing to be happy about, at peace
Knowing life is war, full on hunger and drowning in air
Are they who clearly see there is nothing out there.

Among them you will find that what you want, the way
You want it, is never found. With them you will eat
A most delicious fare that makes hunger itself sweet.

As terrifying to your daily little drama as it may seem,
There is in fact a superior alien life living itself here
In our midst, a nameless wild one who never takes sides.

There is no love among people who think they know
Who they are. There is no joy is this brainy sphere.
Let all beings rot who have determined what they want.

We will meet every morning and evening at the origin,
For coffee and wine supplied by memory of the unmet,
A waitress whose very sleeves smile at the thought.

Though sorrow fills galaxies and fear is faster than time,
Once we arrive here there is none who can longer resist
The terrible desire, the deathly will to become perfect.

VI

Killed by the blue of your eyes, my sigh split the spheres.
It was all perfectly natural, yet cannot be described
Without starting to sound like a crazy drunken lover.

Saying what my heart prompted me to was then not
Enough to say what it prompted me to. But the heart
Likes to trick us into crying over truth, as we all know.

The blue was, is, like an indeterminacy of air and water.
How and why did it impress itself so perfectly on me?
Do provide the science of color I need to speak with you.

If you inhabit air and water, then I am fire and earth,
Something burning with alchemical desire to birth
A new world from the ashes of our cooling pyre.

Burned with you for heresy I would be, drowned in flame
Of dangerous inordinate doctrines. Whatever it takes
To intensely not graduate life with a degree in theology.

In order to take you with me I remained behind forever
At the moment we parted. Such is the lovely illogic
Of impossible goodbyes, a dialectic God and fools grasp.

I might as well say it. In that moment your blue eyes
Pierced me with a radically pessimal hope: that this life
Will indeed, impossibly and inevitably, be our very last.

VII

If the moon appears tonight I will not speak as before.
I will not ask what she is doing up there, all alone,
Or what her gaze reflects upon down on the dark earth.

Her answers I know already. They are the same I provide
Myself, and no one wins that argument, especially me.
So I will ask the moon something wholly unheard of.

A question no one has ever posed, from no perspective
Or angle, from no position of man, beast, or angel.
A question her bright dead body might itself feel.

The question is and cannot be asked. When I ask it,
The question is not. Again her pallid virtue goes to show
That the best thought can do is squirm in its own tomb.

At least we know that nothing wants to be, that all faces
Actually glow and shine with the unspeakable syllables
Of their own intolerable impossibility, that all faces lie.

At least we know that our suffering is real, that sighs
And tears and piercing secret pangs are all that hold
Us together, that sorrow gives something solid to go on.

Not that I actually care whether or not this pain is true,
Only that I would kill myself without it, that existence
Would be a drag if this heart wept not with our moon.

VIII

The trail of severed heads and crushed hearts following
Our axiomatic sigh points the way to who knows where,
Into the new black clarity of an optimally worst oblivion.

Grind the hearts to dust and hang the fresh heads to dry.
Mix the dust with tears to make a mortar for the heads.
Worry not which way the faces go. This work is our road.

The secret of walking is that it need not go anywhere,
That it moves by discontinuing itself every moment.
How pleasant it is to walk together and watch our feet.

To see our paces feel the cobble skulls, to trod the faces
Underfoot and trust the concrete will always hold us up.
How lovely to stroll the dead city atop our own heads!

No one stops working until all brick or stone is replaced,
Until all that glues things together is the solid bond
Of broken hearts. Bless the handiwork of cephalophores.

No one is allowed to go anywhere else until the whole
Metropolis is built anew into the living image of what
It already is: a lifeless city, the very kingdom of death.

Then we will finally know where our first sigh goes,
Then we will see for ourselves by following it forever
Along the lanes of this city, our beautiful last home.

IX

Across the crosswalk I found you, and even then I wished
That we would never move forward to meet, staying
There, gazing still in glad silence across the crosswalk.

Black and white you wear because your mind is zebra,
An open camouflage of impeccable logic, an animal
Game of chess that no one else will ever deserve to win.

People show their true colors at the crosswalk, how
They comport themselves, falling behind or playing
For position. What a bunch of suckers we all are.

That mankind has severely lost step with itself is obvious
By how people walk, lurching and dragging themselves
Forward with the sick gravity of self-important beings.

That this world never was, is, nor will be our home
Is obvious from how we really feel at interstices
And intersections, how we all secretly style our steps.

Smiling there for a long time into your eyes seems
The perfect and only way to really touch your feet,
To lay my head on the cool pavement next to your shoes.

And now, because we failed to do what the heart wanted,
I often pay the price of remaining there, alone among
All the other losers who elect to go along with this life.

X

Because the kind of monastery we need does not exist
On this planet, the globe itself is becoming our cloister,
A capacious secret sphere forever lost in outer space.

Almost nothing is our rule, almost no one will join us,
When it comes time to actually escape it is good to find
That one's true companions are few, very very few.

You asked if there are mystics today in the world
And I answered reasonably. An unreasonable
Question which deserved a less reasonable answer.

Francis rightly disallowed commentary on the rule.
We will secret our *forma vitae* in commentary per se,
Upon the unknown felt text all thought glosses.

There is nothing wrong with being misunderstood
Or misinterpreted. We insist only on honesty,
We demand only the violent rigor of rational love.

From balconies higher and higher we will peer down
On the latest churches and glass spires, perching
From new pillars sprouting atop the tallest tops.

Up here the stench of being human means nothing.
Here where each touches all touchlessly, we watch
The great eye of sincere will melt the earth like wax.

XI

My body will sometimes assume odd shapes because
My heart is constricting itself to hold the worm of
My soul as it twists anew through the human U-turn.

The sky is bruising our toes and the air starts to swim
As I stand up again in the grass and am suddenly
Seven thousand feet tall like Lady Philosophy.

The entire city is trapped within the dream of itself.
This is what architecture is: the construction of signs
Illegible, everywhere reading *One Way* and *No Way Out*.

The stones of buildings are happy here because man
Leaves them alone long enough to return to their nap,
Which makes them stronger, even while decaying.

Everyone knows death is the habit of life, body the
Excreta of soul, and the whole universe God's feces.
Our new hunger tastes the sweetness gnawing the all.

The infinite source of everything is finding a way
To use your mouth to eat itself into the most delicious
Possible meal. You are officially invited to the feast.

But I beg you like a starving pauper to pay no attention
To the contortions of my slippery tongue. Part of me
Is still a poisonous snake and might lead you astray.

XII

Breathing in this world is no longer possible. So I dreamt
Finding two pill bottles labelled with your name, red
And blue, for inhalation and exhalation, respectively.

These pills must have been made from condensations
Of your breath, from sighs and gasps secretly gathered
By little gnomes and sprites in the dream worlds.

There must also be witches and unicorns and deer
And dragons and porcupines and rabbits and flowers
In that world, for the bottles were decorated with them.

Taking two a day is making my breathing easy.
That is, the dream allegorized the becoming-breath
Of your name and the becoming-name of your breath.

Now the medicine is running low, unfortunately faster
Than it might ever be fashioned, much less found.
Even to supply this much you are aeons older than I.

And so the thought of this makes me more addicted
To what I know cannot last, causes me painfully to see
How preciously and pretentiously I waste my breath.

Today I start cutting the pills in two and in two again
As long as life lasts. For I see no other hope in being
Able to tolerate, to even survive, ever breathing again.

XIII

What insanity first caused the sleeping abyss to stir
And drift so far from itself into this vast nothingness,
Depriving forever all things of its perfect, primal rest?

What kind of mad whim might have seized that ocean
Immemorial and pure? Who lead that depth to follow
The irreparable, unforgiveable folly of creating this?

Far vaster than space-time is the mystery of sleep,
A singular impossible thing that everything does
Without having the slightest understanding how.

In sleep's intelligent stupidity and stupid intelligence
I see the infinite dark image of our most original curse,
A truest sign of all that was, is, and will be wrong.

If only I might fall asleep without falling, go to sleep
Without going, sink into sleep and still remain awake.
If only I could truly sleep, like a man, and not a beast.

Then would I wake life itself and surely see at last
The first stir of terrible ignorant desire that once
Sent the All reeling in sick joy across its own expanse.

But it seems that this sight must not be fated for me,
Is not provided to man, whose narrow gaze, seeing only
What it wants and never what is, cannot pass this gate.

XIV

The proud seriousness of their so-called understanding
Is intolerable. I despise it more than anything, more
Even that my own despite, which I despise above all.

Who do they think they are? These Ulyssean charlatans
Of knowledge and experience, who imagine thought
Can map and navigate the Now's imponderable chaos?

What maggoty mania infects their cold wet brains
That they talk the way they do, boring the universe
And not showing the decency even to blaspheme it?

So horrid is their confident, constant blabbermouthery,
So totally insane, that to censure it from existence
Would transform even this infernal pit into paradise.

This expiring age of man is not the time to increase
The mass of clever ignorance overburdening our minds.
The intellectual task of the present is to preserve silence.

Still I confess love for these lost souls, the philosophers,
For at least they are more like myself than the others
And occasionally almost capable of true bewilderment.

I love and pity them in my continual sorrow, in despair
That life permits not, will not for some reason afford me
The tremendous joy of chopping off all of their heads.

XV

The meaning of the Fall is not that man was punished
For sin, but that the human is an animal born incapable
Of paradise, that Eden cannot be Eden if you are in it.

You and I know this, which is why we stay apart together
Far beyond the spheres and why my blood secretly burns
For you in the fire that is melting more than all the stars.

You and I know this, not only in our words, but more still
In the manner we speak them, in the styles of drowning
Silence so deep that one must deny it simply to breathe.

You and I know this because we see that poetry is death,
The floating tomb and supreme grave whose entering
Is exit into the absolutely intoxicated crystal oblivion.

All of the saints were sinners, especially the best ones.
Holding hands in absolute self-defiance, let us carry
The broken vessels of our heads down to the dark joy.

Along the way, this conversation maps our exit strategy.
As one of us is becoming too great for the net to hold,
The other becomes tiny enough to swim out the holes.

Soon to leave for that profound summit, how sweet
It now suddenly is to linger in sad longing, looking
At each other and telling all the galaxies how to move.

XVI

This universe is the best worst of all possible worlds.
It is a shadow, a blackness, a place of derelict sighs
So horribly dead that even the darkness has a face.

We drift with white moons long abandoned by no one,
Waiting to scream inside corridors of excavated time
Where even our reflections become sensitive to pain.

Nervous the cosmos is, and hyperstrung, its physics
A pathetic fallacy of impossible affects contradicting at
Once all directives seeking to subdue its maze to sense.

Being nothing but an overwhelming presence of what
Is never there, this universe is most truly a tomb,
A vast graveyard of itself suspended in nowhere.

Never again bother asking yourself how you ended up
Here. Never again try to steal the show by despairing
That you were born. Neither you nor the cosmos care.

Priests say the crucifixion darkness lasted three hours.
The nature of hypocrites is to pretend things are better
Than they are, to turn what never stops into a story.

Face it. It is no good trying to wake from this dream.
All paths to escape are part of the prison, all roads
Lead to one dead end, a mirror, the nightmare itself.

XVII

Were the pain of my heart any less I would lose hope.
Like a snake it constricts my core, feeding on sighs
Which otherwise would be wasted to the world's air.

Joyfully I nurse this coiling thing, parasite from beyond.
It is an entity more real and alive than me. And there is
Simply no returning to the way things were before.

Or maybe the heart itself is the alien, a fossil thing
Frozen in a distant, polar ontology, until one day,
Unthawed, it expands to destroy whoever discovers it.

Do not discount what causes you to melt and turn pale.
Never presume the deadness of what desire itself desires.
True archaeology illumines its own life as empty tomb.

Only the lustful consume and destroy what they want.
Lovers give themselves to being eaten by the beyond
Of being, to burning in the total holocaust of pronouns.

Among their ashes one always finds unknown elements,
Non-manipulable devices, wholly new prepositions.
In their ashes is never found what you already know.

Doomed are they who fail to fall prostrate before this
Heresy. Forever in hell are any who kill this pain, deny
Our anonymous, inhuman, empyrean conspiracy.

XVIII

Mad is the human mind, and obviously unfit to see
Far into the life of things. It is best to chain intellect
To common matters and let whatever remains go free.

In former, happier times, man knew how to unreason
The world, to unsay all things inside the primal void,
To dis-think everything upon moment of letting it be.

In that world, one thought was like a million seahorses
Passing effortlessly through nets of cosmic ratios,
Swarming all dimensions at once in prismatic insight.

Now man has enslaved himself to figuring it all out
Without intention of doing so, to dredging blindly
The ocean bottom and throwing back what is found.

Believe it or not I am with talking with total authority
About *you*, all your perverse concerns, your problems,
All that you name solid components of so-called life.

Because I am talking about me, the lost, the futile,
He who is absolutely incapable of taking credit
For whatever good you may find in these words.

And so I must now take leave of both myself and you,
Must reenter what I never knew: the transparent joy
Of never having been anything other than a fit, a swoon.

XIX

O absolutely astonished and astonishing one, who so
Madly turns this very sky to scalable mountain stone,
Release me at once from everything that will not climb.

At the end of the day, even inexistent wisdom knows
That there is nothing left even for no one here, here
Below in a realm that thinks nothing other than itself.

Scaling the sky I am, one atom at a time, or maybe not.
Upon the infinite alp there is no room for progress,
Only endless opportunity finally to lose all of it—to fall.

Still, bang this little black goat head upon the rock I will,
During the night when the rest of humanity is resting,
Because I know better, because I know they are not.

Infinite unspeakable pleasure I actually find in not being
Able to ever find it. So that even if you are a mere curse,
Which you are most not, I trust you more than myself.

Or so I tell me, in weird silence, while struggling to find
The next infinitesimal foothold, while my four split feet
Are simply not right, not for here or where I want to go.

Alpinists are really the most appalling melodramatists,
As you know. Anything at all that puts me in mind of
Mountain, of a steep place to climb, is music to my ears.

XX

Mind spinning in spiral shipwreck upon this dark sea,
Heartgold sinking deeper into the nameless infinity,
All is lost, and now almost sadly, there is nothing to fear.

Very dear and not dear has been this life. What to say?
Talking about it makes me sick, yet the suprahuman
Silence is too matter-of-factly sublime to not talk about.

This universe would be unbearable if it were real,
If it were anything more than a murder scene,
A place to solve the last mystery of the first birth.

The absolutely insane impossibility of it crushes my skull
Into dust of suns and embitters my song in hues of black.
But I know what is going on, that it is not me talking.

In the darkness, in the nothingness of absent light, that
Which gave into the temptation to exist and called it gift
Is grown in the cave of now to a great stellarvoric worm.

Twisting inexorably beyond every self-limitation,
This serpent will consume itself in endless spiral
Until the only thing left is the unspeakable, the pure.

In the thought of the curve of your smile the whole
Floating cosmos is being devoured in front of my eyes.
In this thought most extremely happy am I to be here.

XXI

To lay my head on the breasts of the saints, to let go
Your body with theirs, to breathe their sighs into
One's heart and with one's own eyes receive their tears.

To fall into catacombs of friends, to rot sweetly
Together unto a fragrant mass, to be decapitated
In the gentle company of a few companions.

To inhale the incense of your burning corpse
To drink the hot wine of our blood, to find
Oneself over a last meal of human heart-meat.

To never stop being consumed by the interminable
Excess of your own hunger, to remain as one
Forever drunk on the wine of the invisible.

To rant like one possessed, to disgrace
Everyone with the blinding chastity
Of your own marvelous nakedness.

To twist space-time around this body,
To unwind your own umbilical cord
And accelerate the final contrition.

To float in the cloud of unknowing,
To wrestle this blind nothingness,
To lay one's head on a saint's breast.

XXII

Yesterday has passed and tomorrow too. No time is
Left for us, this much I know. This much I clearly see
By the moon's setting this morning beyond the window.

Outside all is calm, without history for a few unwitnessed
Minutes. Thank God people cannot prevent themselves
From sleeping, from opting out of their sick insomnia.

I wish a sleep greater still would fall upon the planet,
Turn the blue earth into a vast floating tomb of slumber,
So deep that waking would induce permanent amnesia.

Then we might be done with all owning and begging,
With the rampant idiocy of protestors and policemen,
All the intolerable terroristic evil of the do-gooders.

Then poet and philosopher would freely kill each other
And a more glorious final war spontaneously spiral into
Paths of violent charity passing beyond the spheres.

For now, somewhere out there you too are sleeping,
Heedless of my early thoughts. Or perhaps you are not,
But awake like me, losing life to pointless contemplation.

However you are, I hope that your happiness is greater
Than mine. At least that gives me something to cling to
In the senseless, boundless enormity of inexistent time.

XXIII

Today you will be with me in the paradise of never
Having been. Today we mount the cross of ourselves,
Bask for three black hours in requiem of the spheres.

Do not ask what we are doing here. No more seek why.
Whatever illumination we need is provided by the stars
Which scourging and buffeting shoot off in our heads.

Like dying of fright before the final blow is struck,
So we die of joy, leaping in horror out of ourselves
Before stepping anew into the absolute enclosure.

More than blood, sweat, and tears flow out of us.
From our three navels sprout a new fourth world
Outside matter-life-thought, above the count of time.

Having seen the irreparable wrongness of all things
Having known there is nothing to be done about it,
We realize at once there is absolutely zero to fear.

Yesterday we were as insane as you, actually thinking
We had to stand! What bliss to be inverted around
The empty point, to be a hook upon which all hangs.

Today I will be with you in the paradise of never
Having been. There we will sport upon the crosses
Like birds plucking out the sweetest eyes of God.

XXIV

Now that you are born human and know how to walk,
It is high time to see that you are an upside down tree
And not at all a man, that you will die without planting.

Dig a hole in the whole earth, make it one huge hole.
Leap like a bird into the air and with new lightness
Turn at top of your leap into a direct head first dive.

Drive your head into the center of the earth. Fall head
First into the core of this whole obscenely deep muck,
This heavy stone mud. Be sure it plugs all the holes.

Make sure the black mire seals your eyes and fills your
Mouth. Fall so hard the very earth enters your little ears
And snakes all the way up into your overused nostrils.

Totally cover and cake your head in earth. Glue yourself
To the earth with your heavy, thick head. Let this facing
Of the total dark earth drive you mad. Bury your brains.

Now let yourself hang from the planet by your neck. Let
Everyone and everything do to your suspended body
What it wants without you having any say whatsoever.

Watch in absolute blindness as your whole body grows
Beyond this world. Watch as your hair sprouts roots
That go everywhere and have nothing to do with you.

XXV

Fiery icicles of our sighs are slowly melting into tears—
Another order of weeping totally unknown in this world,
Another order of world totally unknown in our weeping.

Caves of crystal cosmos now wander within themselves
Like lost children. All eventual tragedies here cry inside
Intense non-existence—instant massacre of all whys.

The nails that pierce my palms are in more pain than I.
The eclipse of our pupils hastens a kind of earthquake
Of the spheres. All saints stand in their tombs and faint.

What has never been me has waited all time for this.
My happiness that it is happening by my never having
Happened is so eternally and infinitely multiplied.

Not only do I intuit how it is for you, not only do I see.
The direct non-thought of it points all in that direction,
Perfuming space itself with unmistakable sweetness.

How could it ever have been otherwise? How might
Anything ever not know anything about everything
That in one moment is happening to you and me?

Without sinking into the dread pit of praise I proclaim
To all dying stars the absolute perverse ineffectuality
Of something that would try once to speak your name.

XXVI

Strange the unshakeable feeling that you are in my body.
So weird that severing is making for such sweet joining.
Uncanny no one ever told me that distance is your skin.

Others run all over the world losing time trying to touch,
Pretending to own the place, as we, stunned by nothing,
Are place itself in constant still wrestling and blind play.

The lump in my throat starting to grow when you played
That beautiful song has engulfed all stench of man,
Composting life itself in an ever-expanding dark globe.

Swept off these feet by a sheer *contemptus mundi* which
Has nothing whatever to do with us, we the inexistent
Now sport in pure foam, the salty surf of indifference.

I am looking forward to the day when the world asks us
What happened. I am destroyed by looking forward to
Being then even more ridiculously unable to answer.

The silence I have learned from your ears is like a little
Insect that now lives in my heart, trapped in a cosmos
More and more surchaotic, safer from itself each instant.

Today something new will happen, again. As if I care.
As if we are concerned in the least with anything
That goes on in this universe, this inquisitorial void.

XXVII

The intolerable cacophony of the world has again begun.
It is spring, and now, because the winter was so eternal,
None will recover from this mad music of sunny lament.

Let the wailings of grey sparrows submerge all seven
Spheres, let tractor beams of lithic sighs draw God to
Earth in multivolume fugues of telluric organwork.

Nothing can survive this singing—a vernal apocalypse
Melting faces with electric eye, converting all minds
To affective pulp in the total sheer grandeur of its gaze.

You do not have to lift your limp eyelids very far to see
That the whole cosmos is totally insane, not to mention
The human world, which never even had a mind to lose.

You do not have to listen very long to know for all time
That no one is here. The mere way anything talks gives
All away, shows that each entity is no more than fear.

You do not have to think very hard about individuation
To perceive that nothing was ever born, to grasp the time
Of life as one massively unknowable single conspiracy.

How it troubles my heart, then, to consider where all this
Music comes from, to think with the silent light of stars
Long since dead, from whence all this terrible sound?

XXVIII

A firing squad of all the mystics who ever lived takes aim
At the head of anyone who even thinks about misreading
Our book, who imagines this text is somehow for them.

My secret to myself, my secret to myself—woe is me.
Because all the sorrow in the world is nothing, nothing
Compared to the pain curious wits will suffer if they pry.

Your vanity is abominable, dear reader, to be despised
Even more than yourself, more than the entire world
Which will never ever understand anything of our love.

Cease to imagine my intelligibility to you, stop trying
To exit the darkness, the vast unilluminable melody
Of night shrouding the corpse of this word from view.

If you have never experienced this perfect sorrow
Of which I speak, at least that is cause for sorrow
Of a lesser kind, a sort over which you should weep.

If you have never heard of the kind of suffering I am
Dying and want to die from all the more, plug your hears
And run screaming in terror from here as fast as you can.

Anyone with the nerve to assume I want anything to do
With them will spontaneously perish. The name of you
Who alter one atom of my sigh is now stricken from life.

XXIX

Because we put off killing ourselves, something else
Had to do it for us. Since I failed to number my sighs
Someone has arrived and is calling me to account.

Now a man we unsought is here, standing suddenly right
Behind your skull, commanding I bow my head to none
So that his sword will unveil more easily the final blow.

Bend your necks my noble ones, my lovely aristocracies
Of one! Rise lowly in love so that your proud crests will
Alight like a flock of bewildered fowl into this dust.

No longer linger for one second on this shore. May not
Less than one more breath pass before we greet each
Other as before in old voices rising from bodies new.

Do not worry about me. It is not that I seek more life,
Only that within three days, whether anyone escapes
Or not, none of us will be ourselves or anyone else.

The time is soon when I return all gold to the thieves,
To the promethean hearts who stole the real treasure,
Whispering this spirit out from the prison of my sighs.

Because we did not kill ourselves yesterday, we are now
Doing so today. It is no joy, but I can conceive of none
Higher than this being pregnant with the death of birth.

XXX

A saint does not die without first silencing everything
Within herself. No fading sun ever finds its reflection
In her frozen tears. Her eyes wash away space and time.

As her tears erase the time of space, so her sighs undo
The space of time, leaving the astonishing sun of her face
Through which the invisible cannot stop itself to shine.

I would be born in another age to be a saint's confessor,
To hear the style of her heartbeat and scribe her sighs.
Not to learn the secret, but simply how to live and die.

Only the saints are ever born. The rest of us were never
Here. Look and see how nearly everyone has given up,
Sold experience for sleep and abandoned their lives.

Who swims with them the monstrous abyss of charity,
Paces the lost, remote speeds of their sleepless longing?
Who can follow the sightless acceleration of their least?

Without her help your very best is just another way
To repeat yourself, only another day of sealing your fate:
To die in sleep without ever having known the truth.

Cast your tears and shoot your sighs unto the saint's feet.
Let your hair rise towards her heights. Chance is good
She will not hear, for her station is lofty, beyond worlds.

XXXI

Once, after daylight died and men remembered to forget
Their care in sleep, I left my father's house by moonlight,
Upon a trail to where I had seen a mountain goat, once.

A little black one he was, as if far too high for his age
Near the sharp summit of a very steep and rocky peak.
How lovely alone beneath blue sky in the bright sun!

Tonight I return there, to where I saw him. I cannot wait
To see if I will see him, observe the secrets of his lunar
Sport, know my full delight in this asymmetrical tryst.

Suddenly he is here! Right before me on the bare silver
Trail, begging me chase him surprised up the mountain.
I breathlessly follow the sure sign of his bright dark tail.

Until something makes my chamois turn quickly back
And run toward *me* with stamping leaps. Afraid I fall
Aside, only to see him trample where I stood—a snake!

Extra happy and excited now, fast as liquid metal flows
Downward he pursues me following him up the mount.
I cannot believe the fortune of our playing together here.

How at the summit do I not find him? Only a line
Of blood to—mirabile dictu—his severed head. Nothing
Killed my *capra neagră*. With his white face at dawn
                    I am free to never return.

gnOme is a secret press specializing in the publication of anonymous, pseudepigraphical, and apocryphal works from the past, present, and future.

"As with music and eroticism, the secret of successful mysticism is the defeat of time and individuation" (EMC).

gnOme is acephalic. All profits from print sales go to the writers.

GNOMEBOOKS.WORDPRESS.COM

Made in the USA
Charleston, SC
16 May 2014